Am I Normal?

Am I Normal?

Illustrated by Afzal Khan
Cover designed by Claire Linney

Am I Normal? US English edition

© C.R. Draper, 2020

Published by achieve2day, Slough, UK

All rights reserved. No part of this book may be reproduced in any form or by any electronic or mechanical means, without permission in written from the copyright owner.

ISBN: 978-1-909986-59-6

"You're not normal," said my friend, Mike.

I tried to find a normal person, so I could see if I was normal too.

I saw my friend, Ruby. "Are you normal?" I asked.

"No, I'm not normal, my name's Ruby. Not many people have the name Ruby." "I like your name," I said and moved on.

I saw my friend, Sunita. "Are you normal?" I asked.

"No, I'm not normal, my dad owns a big company, not many people have a dad who does that."

"Your dad's great," I said and moved on.

I saw my friend, Indi. "Are you normal?" I asked.

"No, I'm not normal, I'm too tall to be normal. Not many people are as tall as me."

"I like you just the way you are," I said and moved on.

I saw my friend, Dave. "Are you normal?" I asked.

"No, I'm not normal, I'm too short to be normal. Not many people are as short as me."

"I like you just the way you are," I said and moved on.

I saw my friend, Layla. "Are you normal?" I asked.

"No, I'm not normal, my little brother has Down syndrome. Not many people have a brother with Downs."

"I love playing with your brother," I said and moved on.

I saw my friend, Alina. "Are you normal?" I asked.

"No, I'm not normal, I have six fingers on each hand and foot. Not many people have that many."

"So, you can count to twelve on your fingers," I said and moved on.

I saw my friend, LeBron. "Are you normal?" I asked.

"No, I'm not normal, I own a rabbit. Most people do not have a rabbit as a pet."

"I love rabbits," I said and moved on.

I saw my friend, Sarah. "Are you normal?" I asked.

"No, I'm not normal, I have red hair. Most people do not have red hair."

"I love your red hair," I said and moved on.

I saw my friend, Kamal. "Are you normal?" I asked.

"No, I'm not normal because I cannot see pictures in my mind. I think in words."

"I like how you think differently," I said and moved on.

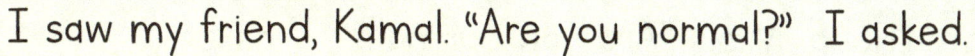

I saw my friend, Max. "Are you normal?" I asked.

"No, I'm not normal, I have five brothers, not many people have five brothers."

"Your brothers are fun," I said and moved on.

I saw my friend, Musa. "Are you normal?" I asked.

"No, I am a twin. Not many people have a twin."

"You always have a friend," I said and moved on.

At the end of my journey, we met at the park. "I didn't find any normal people," I said.

"Who would want to be normal?" Sunita asked.

"Not me," said Ruby.

"Not me," said Max.

"Not me," said Indi.

They all nodded in agreement.

"Why do you not want to be normal?" I ask.

"Because it is fun being different," said Kamal.

"Yes," said Layla.

"Yes," said LeBron.

"Yes," said Dave.

"I like being me," said Musa.

"Am I normal I asked?"

"No," said Sarah.

"Why not?" I asked.

"Because your friends are too interesting."

"That's true," I laughed.

"I like you just the way you are too," I said as I closed my eyes and I snuggled up to her.